God, the Cat and I

Memories of the Past and Hope for the Future

By

Linda L. R. Bennett

LifeRich PUBLISHING

LifeRich Publishing is a registered trademark of
The Reader's Digest Association, Inc.

LifeRich Publishing books may be ordered
through booksellers or by contacting:

LifeRich Publishing
1663 Liberty Drive
Bloomington, IN 47403
www.liferichpublishing.com
1 (888) 238-8637

Scripture taken from the King James Version of the Bible.

ISBN: 978-1-4897-2815-9 (sc)
ISBN: 978-1-4897-2816-6 (e)

Print information available on the last page.

LifeRich Publishing rev. date: 02/21/2020

CONTENTS

INTRODUCTION

T HIS BOOK IS a memoir of a marriage – perhaps somewhat unusual. The following recollections (not all memories are included, only highlights of events) reflect the combined lives of two people. In essence this marriage became a blending of two separate lives to become one life of mutual respect and love. Was it perfect? Absolutely not! Each of us retained our own personalities, including faults and expectations, but we both learned to grow from the strengths of each partner, without forcing change on the other. Both of us were strong-willed and we had no reluctance to express our thoughts. However, over the years, the differences became fewer as we formed a firm bond that transcended our individual wants.

Thus is the premise of this story. The story is especially intended for the family we cherished and, because of God's grace, recounts the "roads" we encountered along our way. The key to this marriage is summarized in one word – commitment. Together we developed a cohesiveness which sustained us throughout the many years.

In the Beginning...

THE SUMMER AFTER completing the freshman year in college, I worked at Southeast Missouri Hospital operating the elevator for staff and patient visitors. This was not a stimulating job but it afforded some money in a clean, stress-free environment. John was doing an internship, following medical technology training in St. Louis, at the hospital. He was one of my elevator customers. A normal day for me primarily consisted in transporting people to designated hospital floors for patrons to see family and friends or for staff to perform patient procedures. Communication was not part of the work day. However, one day, as he was riding the elevator, John started to laugh about a comic which was in an opened magazine that I had been reading. From that point we started talking and eating together in the hospital cafeteria. Ultimately he asked me to go the movies. (At the beginning, one could say, we had an up and down relationship).

After viewing a bad version of HUCKLEBERRY FINN, on our first official date, we took a long drive around Cape Girardeau. We critiqued the film but the conversation became more serious with the passing minutes. John conveyed his ideas about the future. He relayed aspirations and possibilities for himself: Should he go on to medical school, which had been encouragement from those at the medical technology school, or should he think about marriage and a home which he desired because his parents divorced when he was only seven years old? I was perplexed. I had never had such a compelling discourse from someone on a first date, but John's openness, passion for life and his transparency intrigued me

Ensuing days followed the date: the county fair, more movies, Wibb's Barbeque (John's favorite food), long drives, extensive talks, and anything which required little cash (after all, we were just beginning life, the exception was Russell Stover chocolates which John frequently bought for me), became numerous occasions to learn about each other. Shortly John made his decision: he wanted to get married and soon. I was more reticent about such a decision. Nevertheless he was determined; I was the one for him and he saw no reason for waiting. For me, I was enamored because I recognized his intelligence, enact goodness and zest for life – characteristics of what I believed to be a good person.

We married the following November. After John's traditional asking my Father to marry me and notifying the other family members, we exchanged vows at First Baptist church in Cape Girardeau, Missouri. My sweet Mother made a beautiful white satin gown for me. I carried a white Bible topped with a white orchid surrounded by white ribbons. A friend, from college, Eve Lesem (dressed in pink) was maid-of-honor and Jon Lufcy (John's friend) was best man; ushers and candle lighters completed the wedding party. We were ready to begin a lifetime together. John even orchestrated an early honeymoon getaway but there was a glitch: I did not have the key to my home and we had to wait for my Mother and Dad to unlock the house door.

Nonetheless we left for our brief honeymoon anticipating what would become an over fifty-year adventure.

THE IMPOSSIBLE DREAM...

AMID FREEZING RAIN at Paducah, Kentucky, leaving the beautiful autumn leaves in Tennessee, our chosen honeymoon destination, we embarked on a venture of a lifetime. In spite of the weather, we safely arrived to our little efficiency apartment - our first home together. With the promise of a future, dreams and confidence in ourselves, we truly believed all things were possible. Life was just waiting to unfold and we were ready to embrace whatever came our way. We knew we could take on everything.

We both began working our jobs soon after returning to Cape; John resumed his position at the hospital and I took a little seasonal job at a gift shop. Christmas was only a few weeks away and we wanted to be ready to share our earnings by giving to each other as well as to our families. The Christmas tree (bedecked with blue lights, artificial red berries and assorted ornaments) was tiny but perfect for the apartment. Gifts were selected and wrapped. Life was good – soon we learned how a new event would permanently change our life-focus in such a miraculous manner.

We never anticipated that our first year of marriage

would expand to include a little one. Certainly children were part of the future but, as with so many young couples of our generation, our family would begin within that year. Never fear - we were on our way to make multiple changes and unforeseen challenges. Preparations followed as we moved toward the birth of our baby. The expected baby was a new reality as we forged the months before us, apprehensive but also excited. Then she was born, beautiful and perfect.

We adapted amazingly well. Oh, we had spats and not a lot of money - after all this was our first year- but we did not rely on family. We skimped (John even sold some of his blood to the blood bank in order to purchase a cameo necklace-earring set for me in order to celebrate our first wedding anniversary) wherever we could; provision was always available even though we pretty much lived paycheck to paycheck, a pattern which became a lifestyle for years. Immediately we adored our little girl, Dawn Denise (I selected the first name and John chose the second). We were beginning to establish a real family unit, no guidelines for marriage or parenting. We just learned to do it all.

We remained in the efficiency apartment for a few more months but space was getting a bit crowded. Another couple, the fellow was a colleague from the hospital lab, were moving. Therefore, since the facility they were leaving was larger than ours, we relocated to a different apartment. Little did we know, at the time, we were facing new developments - another baby and, in addition, John took what seemed to be a better job, in a Herrin, Illinois hospital lab which meant we would move from Cape Girardeau - we would be truly on our own, no families.

We survived the move. Tracy Lynne (again, I choose the first name, John the second) came one year and six days after Dawn, as precious as the first baby. Days and nights were busy, to say the least; lots of laundry, food preparation for everyone, playing and seeing to the well-being for all of us filled each moment of time. Nonetheless we learned to adapt – we even had a Christmas tree that year in our apartment with Santa coming for our baby girls. But there were hurdles we encountered: The Bay of Pigs occurred that autumn creating a feeling of uncertainty in our world (I remember placing my babies to bed the night that JFK announced the crisis and praying for all of us), winter came and our babies and I were sick with a stomach bug (I called for help while John was working; the only time I ever asked him for assistance while he was at work), Dawn fell down stairs after seeing a cute puppy on steps below her (John rushed to the bottom before she reached the landing), Tracy found a jar with kerosene/paint in the garage and drank the liquid (her stomach was pumped at the hospital and, at our home; I rocked her all night) .Yes, we survived in spite of some struggles. Nonetheless the road for us was to go another direction.

A Road Untraveled

FARMINGTON, MISSOURI BECAME our next home. We settled into a small rental house, again, facing the unknown but with a fearless resolve. We were growing in so many ways: John had a job at a different hospital; the nation endured the assassination of JFK; our babies were becoming toddlers; moving to another town entailed learning the local culture and people. At any rate, we were continuing to rely on each other and actually maturing as a couple. Christmas came with Santa and everything that it brings (that year we took the little ones to see the elaborate Christmas displays with Santa at Stix, Baer & Fuller and Famous Barr in St. Louis); we made a jaunt to visit family in Cape but Christmas morning and Santa were spent at our home with the little girls (a tradition we followed for years to come). Years later we realized the significance of this move and all that happened with it: those were halcyon days, filled with innocence, wonder and delight.

The few years in Farmington contained so much joy and laughter. We started regularly attending the Baptist Church and, as a result, John and I met many young couples who were starting marriage with little ones (appearing the first year or so after they married) and, as young teachers just out of college (John and I even were able to enjoy a little inexpensive vacation with one couple, the Hopkins. at a teachers' resort which included fishing and an attempt at canoeing). Money was scarce. Out of necessity we found activities in homes, before the children's bedtime, no eating-out but simple, home-cooked, inexpensive food, but oh, so good (however, one night we splurged $20.00 by going out with a couple from church, dinner, movies and a baby sitter). John enjoyed playing basketball with local coaches. Tennis grew into a consummate passion for him which lasted for the rest of his life; chess, including its strategies, presented John a profound new interesting form of enrichment. Board games, cards, church gatherings, coffee and dessert impromptu get-to-gathers were forms of entertainment. But, most importantly, our little girls were with us and the source of our true joy (in the summer months, I loved nature walks with the little ones; also, in the heat of the evening, our house was not air-conditioned, strolls were a regular past time, after baths just before the girls' bed time, as the little toddlers rode and I pulled their red wagon).

My days encompassed home. I sewed most of the girls' clothing except for family gifts (my parents especially bought snowsuits, coats and other things); each season found me at the sewing machine diligently creating little dresses and play pants. Planning meals, shopping, cooking, cleaning, household tasks, but, also, tea parties, storybook reading, playing, arts and crafts (using free paper discards John supplied from the hospital lab) were special days. Naptime provided respite for me and rest for tired active little bodies. John's coming from work was always welcomed for me and the girls – Daddy loved his little girls.

After eating the evening meal, fun for Dawn and Tracy really began. Everyone was energized, including Daddy. "Hop on Pop", jumping, giggling, and other escapades lasted until bath time and bedtime (8:00 p.m.). Two very exhausted girls went to sleep, probably looking forward to another romp (I did the nightly story time and prayers). But, in winter if snow had fallen in the evening, the daylight moments comprised sled riding, snowballs, snow men and lots of rough- housing culminating in multiple soaking-wet mittens; after all the activity, hot cocoa, prepared by me, was awaiting at the kitchen table (I was also in the snow angel business and snow ice cream). Joy and laughter were the fare involving the girls and their Daddy.

During these years John and I embarked on another venture: taking college credit classes at the area junior college. Firstly the two of us began taking classes together, U.S. history and American government (required courses); an older next door neighbor stayed with Dawn and Tracy two nights a week when we were away (she was a special lady). We each squeezed study or paper-writing whenever we could, mostly for me during the girls' napping (once night classes were canceled and we called a couple, church friends, who walked blocks in snow to come to our house to play the board game Clue while our little daughters slept– I baked a Wacky cake for a treat, nice memory). We had this routine for two semesters. The following summer

I went to summer school, English literature and public speaking. Biology, psychology and sociology were next for me with English Comp, algebra, and chemistry for John (I can't remember the other courses). Surprisingly the time sped rapidly – all the while our responsibilities did not waver, especially for our family.

At one point, we realized we had maxed-out in course work at the junior college. I was approaching enough credits for a junior year toward a bachelor's degree. The decision was made for me to finish a college degree first (John and I decided a degree would be a better investment than a life insurance policy). However there was one major consideration – a move.

ANOTHER ROAD

CAPE GIRARDEAU SEEMED to be the sensible institution for achieving the plan. From college attendance before we married, I had a year's credit at Southeast Missouri State in Cape. With the credits accrued at the junior college we could envision a degree for me in a relatively short time – no major cost because tuition and fees were reasonable. Dawn by this time had started kindergarten; my parents (mainly my Mother) volunteered to help with the girls, as needed (Mother and Dad were so pleased that I was going back to college) and Tracy would begin school the next fall. Our lives and dreams were moving on.

The following two years entailed rigorous, intense efforts. John, again, was employed at a local hospital lab but took a couple of night classes as well. I plunged full throttle into academia trying to make every moment of the day, and night count (I typed many papers after the family had gone to bed – not a major fete since I am basically a night person and I could do the late hours) but maintaining a semblance of a normal existence was my concern for family. The multiple day-to-day scheduling and happenings seemed at times formidable but we did it – with the Lord's help in the form of my parents and other ways which were not apparent at the time.

Finally, in August 1968, I graduated (in pouring rain and sweltering heat) with a Bachelor's degree in secondary education, major in art education, minor in library science; John, Dawn, Tracy and my parents were in attendance. There had many obstacles along the way: married women especially, young mothers, were not readily accepted at the college, the physical exhaustion was sometimes overwhelming, and the constant concern for family weighed heavily on my mind. Nonetheless John and I had confronted another road and, again, we were ready to forge ahead.

A few weeks following graduation, a new job was awaiting at Kent Library, at my alma mater. The staff were familiar and I easily transitioned from student to a full-time employee. Working at the facility was a good opportunity that provided invaluable experience but John was ready to advance in the medical technology field.

Dawn and Tracy had finished second and first grades in elementary school. John was active in leadership with the AMT (American Medical Technology); his involvement had initiated in Farmington, both at the state and national levels, and he was recognized for his leadership. We both had accomplished more than either of us had imagined. Now, in order to progress, another relocation was necessary. St. Louis beckoned with its many chances for advancement.

THE ROAD NORTH

L OCATING TO A metropolitan area was a new encounter for me (I had lived most of my life in Arkansas) but John had lived and worked in St. Louis during medical laboratory technology school and was familiar with the surroundings. New positions in suburban St. Louis County began for both John and me; John managed laboratories and I assumed a librarian position at Pattonville High School as Dawn and Tracy attended a Pattonville elementary school. Again, the paths were unchartered but we accepted, without much trepidation, these new endeavors as we had in the past, and went on.

New dimensions from St. Louis and the area enhanced our lives. Opportunities availed in multiple ways: theater, museums, the symphony, shopping, restaurants, the zoo and other avenues for growth, culturally and emotionally. Again, we joined a small church (Dawn became a Christian through the impact of this church) and we became involved in its activities (John enjoyed the St. Louis church league softball and I worked with the youth group; all of our family were part of Sunday school classes). We established routines for dealing with new jobs while incorporating exposures from the area and different interesting people – the road north gave us new vistas.

John continued in the AMT organization showing his capabilities at the state and national levels. He was awarded the top national designation at the Atlanta conference the first summer after we moved. Top-level personnel in Chicago were noticing him for his achievements which resulted in another possible career move (during this time the girls and I went with John to a Denver AMT meeting). Nonetheless we were all basically thriving: the daughters were learning in school and many activities (Girl Scouts etc.), the librarian position was fine (I was pretty adaptable – as long as the family members were doing well, I was all right), John was settled in his position (along with taking night classes at University of Missouri St. Louis) and we had adapted to the different locale (John even miraculously survived an automobile accident on the interstate highway). We were amazed when John was offered something he could not have ever imagined - another road but to another city.

THE ROAD WEST
AND BACK

KANSAS CITY, MISSOURI was our next trek. An offer through the Chicago, national AMT organization headquarters, was presented to John. With a CBS affiliation, the Kansas City Business College administration offered him a job to steer- head a medical laboratory technician program on the school's campus. After some deliberation and consideration, John agreed to go along this very different route. He and I were pleased; his reputation for his abilities were once again noticed.

John began the K.C. enterprise while the girls and I remained in St. Louis to finish the school semester. He came back to our home as often as he could until the end of the school year (once the girls and I flew to see him – the first plane trip for Dawn and Tracy). Nonetheless, to our relief, we were all together at the beginning of the following summer.

John compiled a curriculum and established ground work for the program. Even though he had never before undertaken anything of this nature, there was satisfaction in the development of it all. Again, this was another milestone accomplishment. Now, after the project startup, we were to move ahead and back to where we had been, to the St. Louis area. We had not often back-tracked in the past, but we took the road east.

John assumed a job in a hospital lab. I decided to substitute teach. I made an appointment at the public school administration office building with hopes of an offer. Surprisingly I was asked to do something completely different - team-teaching at an elementary school for the rest of the school year. Even though I had no experience, I took the position which presented a doorway for teaching the next few years. Dawn and Tracy settled into an elementary school. Our family stayed the course and resumed life on another direction. Were there apprehensions? Possibly, but our little family was intact, with resilience that overcame many things. Other unknowns had been faced. We were moving along with the fortitude of the past making the best of whatever lay ahead.

Again, the years in Crystal City/Festus afforded much. Membership in the Baptist Church kept us growing in faith and meeting other people (Tracy became a Christian in the ministry of the church) through Sunday school and John played church league softball (however, at the beginning of one summer, he broke his leg while playing a game, resulting in an interesting dilemma because he couldn't drive for a few months while his leg was in a cast). John's tennis skills increased to an all-time level, creating participation in local and other competition (as a result he became the "token" high school tennis coach which helped a young man go to college on a tennis scholarship, to John's delight). For me, teaching became a full-time occupation: first, team-teaching; second, I took a self-contained classroom (fifth grade, with an understanding I would have to take hours for elementary certification if I continued at that level – I decided against the option) the next year; the third, at the middle school, I completed the semester after a teacher resigned; and, lastly, administration asked me to teach art, part-time, at the high school which I did until John had other plans (the principal seemed genuinely disappointed when I resigned – he told me if ever I wanted a position in the district I could have one, nice offer).

John was given an opportunity with a laboratory supply company, again, through contacts from his AMT involvement. He accepted even though he had no experience in that field; later he realized, because of this job, another path was to follow. Dawn and Tracy now were at the ages to leave elementary school and I was teaching. We had lives in our respected areas but times were changing and our lives were going to progress as well as speed up. As always, John did well in working for this small establishment – a new experience, which would later create a different life style for all of us for the years to come, was in the offing - soon.

As we considered our next opportunity, I realized a lot of memories had been collected during the years. I had no emotional ties to the community but our family life was the center for all the main events that really mattered: the surprise Christmas book written by Dawn and illustrated by Tracy for John and me when they were in early elementary school; the "big snow" when school was cancelled for a week before the Christmas break and for about a week afterwards (the girls and I baked lots and lots of holiday treats and they made many melted waxed candles while we were snow bound; John had to walk home, after he parked the car at the bottom of the hill to our subdivision; and the natural Christmas tree which had to be planted in frozen ground – the tree lived); the spontaneous cookouts (hot dogs, chips, marshmallows with chocolate candy bars and graham crackers for s'mores and drinks); the vacation to Philadelphia with side trip to Washington, D.C. (John had an AMT meeting) and other family outings. Leaving the town was bittersweet (we bought our first house in Crystal City) but we left to prepare for the years to come and a provision for better income for all of us.

THE ROAD SOUTH
AND, AGAIN, NORTH

A PERSON, WHO JOHN knew from a variety of sources, contacted him about applying with Abbott Laboratories, Diagnostics Division. After working with the small laboratory-supply company and succeeding, along with other past successes, John seemed a good fit for this Fortune 100, corporation (which had a focus in-line with his previous experiences). In January the company made arrangements for an interview in North Chicago (one of the main corporate headquarters). He made a favorable impression and, after the company's chain of employee scrutiny, he was hired (even though he encountered a difficulty before the main interview – the bathroom water pipes froze at the hotel and John had to thaw ice from a beverage vending machine in order to shampoo his hair). The Memphis area became his first assignment. In the past we always prepared for relocation moves. However, this was a corporate move and there were procedures to follow. We bought a nice house, a moving company (arranged by Abbott) facilitated the packing, etc.; basically our responsibilities involved selling our house in Crystal

City and settling into a new house – everything came together and away we went.

Memphis became our new home. The church we joined had a vibrant, spiritual and thriving youth ministry, perfect for our now young teenage daughters. I savored being close to some of my extended family, my Dad's brother, wife and son, and closer to my parents. We had actually settled quite well when, in just over a year, a corporate move (not uncommon for large corporations) was extended back to St. Louis. We were compelled to move – leaving the promise of a new form of stability; John was doing well in his career change Once more, we made our home in a comfortable neighborhood in the County, close to where we had lived before. The airport was just minutes away, a plus because John was flying weekly for Abbott from St. Louis to various destinations across the country. Dawn and Tracy enrolled as secondary students in Pattonville School District – but this time I wasn't employed fulltime (only as substitute teacher). We found a good church (John became ordained as deacon, a source of pride for us) which was close by. The company benefits provided a comfortable life for the whole family and, for the first time in a number of years I could concentrate on home life; financially John's income allowed us to live securely without my working (also, we felt, since John was travelling so much, I needed to focus on home – and I loved being available for the family). Adjustments were necessary; we did what we had to do.

True to past performance, John assumed his new responsibilities with vigor. Within the first year, after we moved back to St. Louis, he became one of Abbott's top performers resulting in an all-expense trip for the two of us to France (including cash for personal spending). He excelled at corporate sponsored Ohio State seminars, usually out-doing other participants (even some people who had PhDs.). Awards, trophies and symbols of excellence were common occurrences. He relished all that was happening but the pace kept accelerating as he achieved more and more. Nonetheless family was a priority (he telephoned every night he was away) and church was a constant in our lives.

Academics at Patttonville High School accentuated the learning environment for Dawn and Tracy; they were motivated by the accelerated courses offered at the school. Advanced mathematics and science (John's background in these areas was helpful to the girls) and other subjects, along with college credit through St. Louis University, were college-prep opportunities preparing them for college (also both girls were invited to attend the summer St. Louis University Academy of Humanities because of their scholastic success at high school, giving each daughter an additional three hours college credit before their senior year). Educationally the move proved to be a tremendous boost for Dawn and Tracy – they worked hard and they were recognized for their efforts. "If" was not said as John and I discussed college with our daughters but we always used the word "when", again, another goal. Now we could envision the reality of college degrees for both of our children – we were so pleased because another dream was realized.

Family time was always important to us. Saturdays were devoted to activities we could all share. Usually we started with a leisurely breakfast or brunch followed by taking in museums or special local exhibits, shopping at the malls, or movies. During winter months, for supper I prepared a pot of hearty soup served with hot bread and a good dessert; afterward we sat at the breakfast table playing board games or the like. Sundays we went to church and had a traditional Sunday meal with the foods we enjoyed. The weekends were filled with moments to compensate for the busyness of the preceding week. Birthdays, holidays and other special events were reasons for celebration - celebrate we did. Our home life was of utmost importance. Memories of those family days are sweet; even now, I like to relive those happy times in my memory.

Dawn graduated from Pattonville High School in the spring, 1979. She was one of two valedictorians in a class of around eight hundred graduating students. Numerous awards and accolades to recognize her scholarship were given; two parents could not have been prouder than John and I were. College was looming ahead for our first child; she was ready for it in the best possible ways, with scholarships in tow and the educational experiences from high school, to face a new beginning.

The following summer we shopped for everything that dorm life at the university would entail: bed linens, curtains, a trunk, bookshelves, etc. – cozy and comfortable for her home away from home. Lists of necessities, as well as just some enjoyable items, materialized as mountainous stacks in Dawn's bedroom. Our hopes were for her life to be as good as possible for our first born. August, Dawn would be leaving; we wanted her to be ready.

Mid July St. Louis temperatures are usually extremely hot; maybe all the pavement and the Mississippi River accentuate the humidity of sultry days and nights. The summer following Dawn's graduation was no exception. On a Saturday, during July, we attended a wedding at the church when John started profusely perspiring. The family attended church on Sunday, as usual, but late Sunday night or early Monday morning I awakened finding John sitting on his side of the bed. He said, "Linda, I feel like a truck is on my chest." Quickly, not really realizing what was happening, I called the hospital which was close by. I was told to bring him to the emergency room – immediately. Without hesitation, I told John to dress in street clothes as I quickly dressed. I hurriedly drove John to the hospital, leaving the daughters sleeping in their beds. Neither of us had a preconception of what was occurring. We thought the heat was causing his problems. We both assumed he would, after a short time, be examined and released from ER – but the unforeseen occurred, putting a twist to our lives.

Heart attack. After extensive testing doctors determined John had had a heart attack, a mild one but, from the lab tests, he probably was headed for a massive attack in the near future. Major blockages were in two of his main arteries. From the cardio-vascular team, open heart surgery was the recommendation to bypass the clogged arteries. At the time, procedures were in the early stages of development and we now approached something completely alien to us. John was only forty years old in seemingly good health, no cigarettes, alcohol and plenty of exercise (however, in the previous February, there had been some indications of health issues and John had had some tests, after my insistence). We were surprised. Nonetheless, the impossibility was possible. This road block had to be confronted.

Surgery was performed on August 5, Dawn's birthday. John spent the following next few weeks in Barnes-Jewish Hospital, St. Louis. Each day, during this time, Dawn, Tracy and I were en route to the city and spent every day with John. Other activities were on hold; we wanted to be with him. Fortunately recuperation went quite well, in spite of the magnitude of the procedure. John was anxious to return home. Within two weeks he was welcomed back to what was our sanctuary – home – and never was there a happier man. Through all of the situation, church friends, Abbott comrades, neighbors, etc. were so kind to us, from prepared meals, visits, telephone calls, mowing our lawn, etc.; we were blessed. Still our attention was on another way because Dawn would soon leave for the university.

John insisted he go with us when we did the move to Columbia, Missouri – the University of Missouri campus. The doctors, with emphatic cautions, agreed with his request under certain conditions: a back seat conversion-bed (lots of pillows, as comfortable as possible), no stairs at the dorm, and little walking. We embarked on the trip loaded with all the items collected for the move. Cautiously we abided by the instructions. Dawn's dorm room came together with all her things. The quest had been successfully achieved and she was ready for a new beginning. We left – all the way back home I silently cried as I drove the car.

That fall Tracy began her senior year in high school.

Dawn started her freshman year at the university. John, within two months after the surgery, resumed his job routine, flying across the country and, in addition, assumed more responsibilities in the form of a promotion as district manager for Abbott. As far as I was concerned keeping everything going on the home front was enough. All appearances our lives had picked up where we left in August. Certainly changes had happened but, as usual, we were doing what had to be do; the pace had not really been altered. I had some misgivings but kept quiet. We moved on from the pieces of the shattered past events of the summer, in some respects, as though nothing had happened. Again, our family was moving forward. The path was taking twists and turns which had never been navigated.

That year went quickly. Tracy completed the senior year in high school and graduated in May. She excelled capturing the honor of valedictorian of her class of around seven hundred students (only four classmates achieved the recognition). With honors for her academic accomplishments and scholarships awaiting she was directed toward the university the coming fall; her Dad and I relished in the pride for our younger daughter with satisfaction that, in spite of circumstances, we had overcome impediments but our hopes had prevailed.

The summer came with a flurry of activity anticipating the coming fall. There was no less excitement getting our second child ready to start as a university student. Again shopping and purchasing for Tracy's home away from home supplies consumed most of those few months; we wanted life to be good for her while she was away. Then

August came and both of our daughters were taken to the University of Missouri and we began a completely new chapter in our lives.

I had not truly felt the impact of the events of the year until both daughters left for college. At once, reality kicked in and my mind was flooded with "what ifs". John's Abbott responsibilities intensified with his managerial role in keeping many persons under his direction, traveling hundreds of miles each week, mostly flying. Dawn and Tracy, as dedicated students, were focused on their academic pursuits. My Mother and Dad lived at least three hundred miles away. What if something happened and I would be left all alone?

Repurposing my life, as well as keeping important priorities, was something of a dilemma for me. In some ways I had lived vicariously through the lives of my family albeit I had willingly done so; I loved them all and I enjoyed helping in any way possible. But I had to find ways to help them and find fulfillment in additional ways. I cannot say an inspiration was instantly revealed from heaven. However small steps stopped my fears and my pity party subsided.

Our family welcomed opportunities to share our home whenever we could. As an outgrowth I became involved in Friendship International which was sponsored by the St. Louis Southern Baptist Association. Women with worldwide backgrounds participated in the program allowing Christian Americans to assist them in understanding our culture, everything from shopping to comprehending our idioms and unusual expressions in every day conversation (for the most part the women were spouses of graduate students who were seeking advanced degrees from U.S. universities and their command of English was exceptional). Relationships developed as some of the ladies, including families, and I formed a special bond: We learned from each other realizing we had much in common creating open discussions but always measured with respect resulting in gratifying friendships. (Two different summers our family was also asked to host visiting Japanese college girls who had been sponsored by Missouri Baptist University; this gave the entire family enrichment opportunities).

Sometimes I drove to Arkansas to spend time being with my parents. These visits were important for me to monitor health issues (especially my Mother) and to help them when they needed assistance but I treasured simply being with them – after all they were and always had been a major part of my life. However, many occasions, John was able to coincide a business trip and travel with me one part of the journey (I would drive to the Little Rock airport and he would catch a flight to a designated appointment or I would get him from a trip). John didn't really like for me to travel alone, but the alone time became moments for reflection and contemplation which I needed.

Another possibility for growth came in the form of an interdenominational women's Bible study. Many were Baptists, the same as I, but ladies from Lutheran, Methodist, Presbyterian, charismatic, Catholic denominations participated. We were all Christians who wanted to learn from God's Word in spite of doctrinal differences. We did learn and, as an added bonus, the camaraderie among the ladies was truly a blessing.

In the meantime John was advancing with the Abbott career, our daughters were immersed in their university studies and time was swiftly passing. Dawn completed the bachelor's degree and decided she did not wish to apply for medical school (she had studied premed; her Dad was pleased that she had changed plans) but she pursued the Journalism School at the University of Missouri, one of the highest ranking programs in the country. Tracy continued to focus on a pre-veterinarian degree. Fortunately, amid all of this activity, we were able to travel to Europe – as a family, the last family vacation, that became a time for a wonderful memory. Again, our lives continued on with more blessings than we could have ever imagined. But, again, another move was coming.

Big corporations project personnel changes at the beginning of the calendar year. John and I found that was certainly true of Abbott but we had not been required to relocate due to John's persuasiveness about staying in St. Louis. However, during the fall, upper echelon management informed him he had a choice of three locations where we should move: Cleveland, Pittsburg, or Memphis. Because of our familiarity with the area and somewhat proximity to where we were living at the time, we chose Memphis. Whatever the choice, we were faced with a move that would place more physical distance from our daughters – an overwhelming thought and one that made the move very difficult (at least, during the years with Abbott, John never pursued an international appointment, which could have been a possibility because of his excellent Abbott performance – many calls came from "headhunters" who were interested in hiring him for similar corporations; his reputation as an achiever became well-known).

The Abbott moving procedures kicked into gear: the movers were notified, our house in St. Louis was purchased by the corporation, corporate funds were available for John and me to search for a house in Memphis, etc. The mechanics to go forward were in place. However this situation was different because our daughters had always been a part of moves and they would be so far away after we left St. Louis. Mentally I grasped the scenario but I had reservations emotionally and I hated to leave the area. Our family, all of us, had to realize one of life's hard lessons: change is an absolute, sometimes regardless of feelings.

During the final processes of leaving our St Louis home, memories of the last years engulfed the house. I was comfortable with our lifestyle. In spite of insecurities which developed with John's health we had adapted and we had become familiar with special people, church, and the advantages given to us. Nevertheless, once again, John and I struck out not knowing what the future was to bring.

CROSSROADS

A GAIN MEMPHIS BECAME our residence. A nice house was found in the same vicinity where we had lived before and, after the movers left, John and I unpacked boxes and arranged our belongings to create a feeling of home. John started the different assignments for Abbott. We attempted to continue our lives but there was a sense of instability about things: John's new position entailed more driving (we had thought he would travel less but he was away as often as he had been when were in St. Louis; also a colleague who worked under John had a heart attack at motel while he on the job and was clinically dead before he was revived – something of an ominous warning for John). Major reevaluation of what we were doing became eminent. We knew we needed to go another route. Again, with no precedent, our thoughts became focused on untraversed possibilities - we truly faced crossroads which would take us in unchartered courses, something like Sara and Abraham did during early Biblical accounts.

John and I had no guidelines to follow as we made our choice on another course. There were a lot of road blocks to this venture: John would quit the position with

Abbott; we would have to sell the house in Memphis and purchase another in the "new" land; family and friends would question our drastic undertaking; and primarily we would had no employment and no the benefits (health insurance, etc.) from Abbott. The whole scenario seemed risky. Nonetheless we stepped out on faith knowing how we had been blessed in the past and we relocated to Batesville, Arkansas – looking toward whatever was ahead.

We moved in February during probably the worst winter storm the area had known in many years. Snow and freezing temperatures made the highways treacherous as we encountered the steep hill entering the town; at one point, descending a curve as I drove following John in one of our cars, the car veered to the left lane of the highway and miraculously stopped on the road's shoulder, with no approaching traffic, and I was able to steer the car back into the right lane. After the harrowing journey from Memphis we were welcomed to the warmth and safety of my parents' home. However the movers did not come with our furnishings for another week due to bad road conditions – this was a wonderful respite and blessing after all the "ifs" of the episodic move and we all of enjoyed the unexpected time together before John and I faced the overwhelming task of reestablishing in different surroundings.

With no job, but with a nice severance package from Abbott and faith, we examined the next steps for our future. Never had we been so bold. Jobs were not available in the area. However, through the acquaintance when searching for a house, a real estate agent impressed us enough to look into a totally untried occupation; thus a diverse road was taken to form an association with a real estate company.

To prepare for real estate practice in the state, Arkansas requires a special license test. With his usual resolve, John took the test and started working. Even though sometimes I was hesitant about this immense, life-changing undertaking but we could not look back. We either had to look forward or languish in doubt concerning our choices; our daughters were doing post graduate studies, Dawn in the master's degree program at the University of Missouri School of Journalism and Tracy in the University School of Veterinary Medicine, and were on to their professional careers (John made the statement that the Abbott position had been the provision to get them on their way). We moved on, one step at a time, not aware of impending events. At the start of this venture we did not realize all of the ramifications resulting from our choice but we never before had known outcomes when we began something new – maybe we would have not attempted as much if we had settled for comfort and security. Now, as in the past, we embarked into the unknown.

After a while John tested for the state real estate broker's license. In the interim he and his business associate incorporated the business as a partnership. These actions seemed to correlate with a conclusion for me: I should become a licensed real estate agent. Therefore I started working with him, after taking the real estate test, and the other agents in the office (I had never envisioned something like this job, a completely alien concept for me).

The following few years brought significant

life-altering happenings. Tennis, once more, gave John an outlet to meet people in the community; there was a thriving network of good tennis players which later proved to be an important opportunity for John. The real estate field, after some months, provided some income. We became involved in church and John in the Rotary Club (he went to a number of conferences, etc. due to his participation in leadership with the organization and we shared our home with individuals who were part of teams visiting from India, Austria, South Korea and Australia; also, one summer, a recently college graduated young woman from Indonesia stayed a month with us). However my Dad's health took a down turn and, after a year of relatively normal life, he died – this was one validation that the move to Batesville had been Providential. John and I had lived here for less than five years; life was directing our attention in ways we had not anticipated but we had to see the challenges as opportunities and continue on.

Curiosity attracted John to an older house which was for sale. Through investigation he learned the property needed little work to become a site for the real estate business. The price was right. With the approval of his partner, the property was purchased and renovation began. John and I could not have undertaken such a project but the partner had knowledge in construction improvements, etc. and together the two created an amazing transformation – a good business and personal investment. After some decorative touches the business was ready to resume.

We did have a lingering concern – no health insurance. We found, after he left Abbott, John's heart medical history was a detriment to acquiring a personal health policy; no company would take him because of his past problems. Interestingly, an answer to our concerns came in a totally unexpected manner: a job for me.

An ad appeared in the local newspaper about a position for a research and development project initiated by the Arkansas Department of Education. On a whim I applied for the position and was hired. The state had received federal grant money to search for ways to help three vo-tech institutions in student recruitment and retention. There were no specifics to follow but the mandate was to create manuals of methods to assist the schools in helping students. Since this job was under the auspices of the state, I (and John) would be provided with a group health insurance policy – a blessing we could have never anticipated (within the two years for the project, John had another heart attack and, subsequently, bypass surgery).

For over two years I traveled to each of the schools involved. I literally became a part of each campus, visiting each one per week observing their procedures, characters and perusing any materials, as well as conducting staff workshops, relevant to my task. In past experiences, never in my thinking would I have attempted such a responsibility but, out of necessity, three manuals, when the tenure for the grant concluded, evolved and were submitted to the state. At this point I was no longer employed; in turn the manuals were produced for ERIC, a national database. A new threshold was awaiting.

The local vo-tech facility needed a full-time librarian. In previous years, library positions had been available for me, at the college level and at high school. Fortunately I was offered the job. Again, a different challenge was presented because the library had little to make it a functioning or viable part of the school, with little financial support and limited existing materials. No matter the opportunity was seized. I started as soon as the research project was completed; thankfully health insurance (for John and me) was part of the state package of benefits.

Even though little was provided, the library took off. Materials were scavenged from every possible source: donated books, newspaper articles, brochures (for a vertical file), discount book suppliers and anything free which provided information for student needs. Eventually enough money was allocated to purchase THE ENCYCLOPIA BRITANNICA and increases were made to expand magazine and newspaper subscriptions. At the beginning everything was managed by me, with a few volunteers, but work study students and, eventually, other staff were hired to assist with what was beginning to form a functioning facility. Finally, space, from existing areas in the building, was incorporated to improve patron accommodation – the library had started to be an important part of the institution even though it had long way to go.

An accreditation was looming for the school. The criteria required a librarian with a master's degree. I did not have one. Therefore, if I wanted to continue, entering a library science program was necessary. Upon investigation, I learned the University of Tennessee was offering courses in conjunction with Memphis State in Memphis, TN. After taking the GRE again (over twenty years had passed since I had taken the test) I applied to the program, going to classes on Friday nights and Saturday mornings for a semester (my aunt and uncle allowed me to stay overnight with them – I was so grateful). However U of T discontinued the offerings. Choosing a closer university which gave the ALA-MLS program had to be found. Arkansas did not have such a possibility, but where could I go?

I applied to the University of Missouri, because it had the closest ALA program, and was accepted. Following three summers (four-week sessions), three semesters commuting to night classes (to Columbia, U of Mo Jefferson City campus and St. Louis Public library in the city) and the grueling final comps I graduated – while maintaining work at the library. The process was challenging, not only for me but for John. However we made it; during this time but Mother died before seeing the completion of the degree, one disappointment for me because she would been so pleased.

In the hurry of the studies, etc., John was appointed to the Arkansas Real Estate Commission, where he served a term as chairman (his involvement allowed him to attend numerous national meetings); he was recognized for real estate sales; his tennis successes developed into coaching at Lyon College; and I settled into the Library Director's position (by this time the campus had affiliated with the University of Arkansas). Our lives had undergone radical change, including our daughters with their careers, marriages and children. We had experienced so much, things gratifying but some loses as well.

In hind sight, all that had happened seemed amazing. The number of years came and disappeared but, in the meantime, we had grown into people we never could have envisioned; basically we were the same but with experiences that made us stronger. We had not always purposed our life journey. Nevertheless a plan had unfolded along the way.

Sometimes, for no logical explanation, we had attempted a direction which was completely opposite from an original intentional path.

A recap of the first of our Arkansas years could be as follows:

* moving during the big ice/snow storm,
* pursuing new modes for making a living,
* preparing ourselves with necessary credentials for the real estate business,
* adjusting to a different lifestyle,
* coping with changes in our families (deaths of family members and dear friends; adjustments to our family, through marriage, etc. and subsequently new dimensions to our lives with the births of Bryan and Kayleigh for Dawn and Brad then Laurel and Heidi for Tracy and Greg – giving a sense of a continuity for promises in years to come),
* seizing the unexpected as new opportunities (new job offerings which necessitated returning to academic studies),
* emerging old health issues,
* beginning anew in previous work-related positions,
* keeping focused on values and priorities.

The mindset of the past was superseded with a "new" reality. We no longer could live by the norms from years before. Sometimes, although unspoken, John and I were overwhelmed by the prospects ahead: what should we do and be as we travel the ever-changing momentum we faced? Nonetheless each day appeared and we trudged taking one step at a time – steadfast in faith and not knowing about the future. Together John and I were really passing from era to era in our lives. Each phase of life required unique circumstances for passage to the following stage without an undefined pathway. We simply kept moving along to some designated outcome which we had no idea was awaiting – serendipity perhaps is a word to describe the path we were doing. Still, we were blessed beyond any logical measure.

The forthcoming years held unexpected drama with unimaginable vicissitudes. The road taken at the beginning of our marriage was unlike the ones we took along our way, especially the happenings as we left middle age. In some ways, because we had been so blessed, John and I, whether we realized or not, assumed we could manage this life no matter whatever might occur. Certainly we had faith to face the unexpected but the time came when one of us had to carry most of the hard choices, a reality for most long marriages - I was the one, in the final stage of our life, to be responsible for most of the choices. The approaching crossroad involved one of formidable and forever consequences which concluded a lifetime journey we had traveled together.

ROAD'S CULMINATION

TRANSITION WAS ANOTHER passage lurking around the corner for us. Even though John had continued both operating the real estate business and coaching college tennis – alone – I recognized he was having difficulty with all the aspects of both tasks and I insisted he quit both jobs. I was fortunate to stay with the library position; I had a monetary goal I thought we needed for retirement. However, since I felt we should spend more time together (signs of decline in John's health were taking toll), one summer, I realized the retirement goal had been met. To further affirm the decision John fell in the breakfast area at home resulting in a profusion of blood loss; if I hadn't been home I think the event could have been life-threatening. Indications were clear. I notified the campus administration I would not return to the library in January at the start of the new semester.

Christmas came with the family – fortunately all of them, both families of our daughters – gathered at our house. Then, as we entered into a new year and in the throes of another "new" beginning, John and I sorted through an accumulation of unnecessary paperwork and possessions from all the many preceding years. We began to catchup on spending time together - eating breakfast at home, taking impromptu car rides, talking with each other more than when I was working, and just doing simple activities. Still there was continued health regression for John. But somehow we seemed to adapt to a somewhat simplified life style and I kept thinking our lives were on the upswing for the most part; we could no longer travel as we had in the past (only short local road trips) but life was proceeding. Then came the following July.

John and I were preparing to grocery shop. Company was coming and everything was about ready, as we anticipated their arrival, with exception of some food items. We were in the process of leaving the house when I abruptly turned and fell (about in the same place John had fallen). I knew I had broken the right thigh bone when I saw my leg. John gave me the telephone to call 911. In a short while we were on our way to the emergency room, instead of putting the final touches for a family visit. John was anxious.

The next weeks presented new problems for us. Life took a downward spiral from which we did not recover. First, for John, was the separation anxiety of my hospitalization; nothing of this sort had ever happened to me in all our marriage. Secondly, even though all went well, there was a recovery time; I simply could not do what I had done before, as quickly. Our family came to our rescue, as well as many friends, but our normal existence was immeasurably altered. John didn't understand, even though physical healing came about earlier than had been predicted; I managed to get around on a walker but I could not walk as I had. Then late summer came.

One morning John and I had finished eating breakfast when he commented about a pain in his chest. Immediately I called our family doctor and was told by the nurse the doctor would not see him – go to ER. Following events created nothing less than a storm for us. We faced chaos and delays before John was found a hospital room. Once in a hospital room, after a time of frustration, his sleep was suddenly interrupted by a technician, with no notification, resulting in John's agitation. In a hurry John was assigned another room – a room where I could not stay during the night. The whole scenario manifested itself into a complete emotional tailspin for John who already was grappling with the situation. At the time I couldn't imagine what the future days, weeks, held but finally, after my persistence, I was able to bring him home for a time. However the damage had been done to John's sense of well-being and calm. He never completely rebounded and our lives were dealing with unfamiliar territory.

During that autumn a semblance of a normal routine was attempted, even though I was still overcoming the broken leg of the summer. Thanksgiving Day with a usual dinner and all the trimmings was celebrated with Tracy and family. Fortunately, the families of Dawn and Tracy converged, once again, to enjoy Christmas with John and me. When everyone had returned to their respective lives, I remember thinking, as John sat in his recliner holding one of our cats as the other two looked out the patio doors while snow was falling, we were going to be all right – life was not the same but we would make a new normal.

At this point in our lives there seemed to be no direction to recapture what we had in the past; every day was quite different from the previous day. Still the days passed from winter to spring and then from summer to fall.

Christmas came once again. Fortunately the entire family was with us. John and I had bought a natural-cut Christmas tree; John, during some shopping, had even selected a nut cracker ornament for the tree. The tree was decorated with our traditional ornaments including strung popcorn and strings of fresh cranberries – there seemed a sense of serenity which is appropriate for the season; he even commented on the beauty of the tree. Still John's persona was not quite the same with agitation and, on occasion, an aura of remoteness.

When spring came we continued a general day-to-day routine, still some shopping and regular life activities, as much as we could. However, that following summer presented a whole array of difficulties. Extreme hot temperatures of the season exasperated and hampered even short outings which we were accustomed to. John's moods plummeted.

He seemed confused and uncooperative. For the most part we remained at our house. Still, in spite of it all, at times John would reflect on the beauty of flowers in the front porch planters, as we sat swinging in the glider. But there were repeated falls inside the house which resulted in more than one 911 call for help to assist me with him. Finally, after one episode when I couldn't get him off the floor, he was hospitalized.

John responded to the medical staff. He started eating and was more alert than he had been for some time. Just when he seemed on the road to recovery, the hospitalist decided John needed to go to a rehab facility. I brought his favorite polo shirt and nice casual slacks for him to wear as he was prepared to be transported. I felt a sense of hope and anticipation as we left the hospital. After we arrived to the rehab the driver, a professional health assistant, said John should be ready to leave in around two weeks. There was a glimmer of excitement and I knew we would soon be back home; we could pick up the threads of life as we had before. But I was wrong.

What I was told to be a period of two weeks developed into a prolonged stay of around five to six weeks. John's condition worsened. I remained with him most of the days but otherwise I attempted to find other ways to care for him at home. I found no assistance from health agencies and especially from the facility's staff – mainly we were stuck in a no win situation (John seemed to be aware of my efforts because once he said, "You are my girl." With tears in my eyes I responded, "I am. I always have been. I always will be." He seemed at peace, no inner turmoil or distress). I simply wanted him home, a place of security and calmness.

Finally, at the end of September, a hospital bed, a wheel chair and health aides became available to help care for John; I knew I couldn't physically do the job by myself. One of the rehab therapist remarked, as we were leaving, that John had been more talkative; I am sure he was anticipating home. Home we went. I arranged for the next door EMT neighbor to wheel John to the bed. Nursing aides came for medical care for five days. I prepared easily-digested food John liked. However I could not arrange for any weekend professional – no one was available to be with us or help to give any assistance.

"AMEN"

DURING THOSE FIRST days, after the arrival at home, a minister, whom had worked with John on civic activities and whom John respected, came to see him. He and I chatted about topics trying to be inclusive but John was silent. Upon leaving an invitation for prayer was offered and the minister prayed. At the end, the minister said amen. Almost immediately he said, "John said amen!" The only word John had spoken since we had come home.

John and I were completely alone for the weekend. There was no one willing to help. I had the total responsibility but I faced what I thought needed to be done preceding with fortitude of the past. On early Sunday evening I had finished serving John broth (he had not been eating much that day) and turned ready to give him his usual medication but, when I attempted to administer it, he was unresponsive. Immediately I called 911. The responding EMT did not find any positive indications but I insisted additional efforts be applied.

I drove behind the emergency vehicle to the hospital ER. I watched the hospital staff for at least an hour as the doctor and nurses tried to revive John. Ultimately all the efforts were to no avail. John's life on this earth was gone. We had begun life's road many years before and he had completed his portion of life with just the two of us and God. The date was October 2. I think the last word John spoke was fitting, "Amen" – so be it

AFTERTHOUGHTS

KNOWING JOHN, I would imagine his memorial service would have pleased him. My only regret was the minister who conducted the narrative of John's life – he really did not know John – what he said, did not capture the essence of John. Nonetheless the honor was given to John, and God's glory was acknowledged through hymns, thoughts, prayers, Scripture verses and John's favorite poetry. I am not sure a summation of a life well-lived can be done in a matter of an hour or so but with the presence of family and John's colleagues and friends the day was significant and meaningful.

The interlude between the service and Thanksgiving seems something like a blur but Tracy and family came for that day and a few weeks later Christmas followed with the blessing of a family gathering – daughters, sons-in-law, and grandchildren. Traditions were alive; even though John wasn't among us, his spirit permeated the activities of the season – a beautifully decorated tree, good food, exchanging gifts, and laughter, as John's photo enhanced the fireplace mantle above his stocking which was hung with all those belonging to the family. I purchased pewter key rings which read "always with you" and placed them in cards (with John's title for the individual written inside) for each person to further accentuate John's memory. Amid a few tears, but with the joy of Christmas, the celebration provided a sense of continuity and an affirmation of the meaning of living life on earth but, also, the promise of everlasting life.

Years ago John had begun compiling items, from all his extensive activities, in a few notebook binders. He told me he wanted the grandchildren to learn of the jobs he had had, church, civic participation, and other areas of his life (including tennis, etc.). I had worked some with him on the project but the task was large. Over two years passed, after he died, I finally organized all the clippings, plaques, and other mementos which had accumulated for over fifty years – filing cabinets, desk drawers, chests, etc. were rummaged to give a semblance of order to the time we had shared in all his multiple pursuits. Determining important objects was arduous but fulfilling. The collection is complete; I believe John would be pleased.

As I look back, our marriage was multifaceted. John said our getting together was a gift from God. How two individuals from totally different backgrounds and personalities melded to form a solid union is something of a mystery. We had very little materially to begin "the impossible dream" (the American dream) when we started. There were various ups and downs as we meandered the variety of "roads" along the ways, stretching both of us and our daughters while we went along. Maybe flexibility, not hesitating to changes and challenges, provided the wherewithal for us to overcome the pitfalls on the journey. Learning to take risks (something I did not do until John and I married) combined with commonsense (John acquired along the way) sustained us during the hard times (and there were those) as well as a little of serendipity (a trait I think accentuates a good life) for strength to our relationship – a sense of humor helped (laughing at faults and failures, reality) through all of it. Whatever the ingredients there were for the marriage, they meshed and worked for us; we had blessed life. As a sideline I learned an important of concept of home: it is not found in a place but in the heart.

Placement of the double grave marker seemed to take forever. The stone we wanted was not available at the engravers when the selection was made. After a special order, the stone size was not correct. Months passed before everything came in place at the cemetery. With persistence and patience, now the marker rests in its proper spot. Personal data for John and me are prominently displayed but, between this information, three words are boldly etched in the stone: love, faith, hope. These words underscore the legacy I believe John and I want leave:

> Love – For God in the persons of the Father, Son, (Jesus) and the Holy Spirit; for our family; for fellow men
> Faith – In our Lord (our Sustainer, Redeemer and so much more); confidence in each other.
> Hope – For the future on this earth but, more importantly, for life everlasting.

The marriage John and I shared was not a fairy tale, not a perpetual state of euphoric bliss; happiness (happiness can be an offshoot from staying the course and not faltering on the trip) was not an idealized goal but dealing with the reality, at hand, along with a blending of tenderness, care and, sometimes, raw courage as we sought more the extraordinary not the ordinary or convenient path. It was a commitment which endured the years among triumphs as well as disappointments. Those last months of John's life were accented with unrecognizable attitudes and frustration because he was unable to do as much as he had done in the past; there were things he still thought he could do as he had before (as illustrated by his wanting to hit some tennis balls on the court but I knew he was unable - I never took him). Through faith, dreams and sheer grit we saw fulfillment in our life; second best, just good enough, or better were not part of our vocabulary, but the best was our aim as we strive to rise above nitty-gritty everyday conditions we faced. At the beginning John and I could have never envisioned what eventually was accomplished. There is bittersweet mixed in all the years. But, during our last months, time after time John expressed his love and said he didn't know what would have happened to him if we hadn't married – nothing more needed to be said (after my Dad's death, my Mother said, "We understood each other." I think I could say the same about John and me).

Sorting through paraphernalia is accomplished. The order of the day is to simplify things and to eliminate clutter. A serenity surrounds me as I move through these months and years. The past contained more than can be completely understood. Whatever special magic we had cannot be recaptured (however, I mentioned, in passing, I would press "replay" for those passed years - if I could).

For now, in quiet moments of each day, I can contemplate what John and I had. Tranquility gives me, in the present, an incomprehensible feeling of gratitude. In perspective, the time seemed to go too quickly, but we filled our lives with purpose. The void in my heart is full. Additional thoughts are really inadequate to express and should not be stated: God, the cat, and I remember: memories of the past and hope for future.

End

APPENDIX

A Compendium of "These and Thats" (Plural for "This and That")

- Immediately, after we decided to marry, John insisted he formally tell my folks. He said to my Dad, "Linda and I want to marry." My Dad responded, "She hasn't finished a college education." "I like her the way she is," was John's reply. However, John's Dad made the most surprising remark as he looked at me when the announcement was given, "Who to, you?" All of us started laughing. I was the only possible person there!

- Jokingly I often reminded John I married him because of his car. By the time we met he had sold his baby-blue Buick convertible, which he had purchased with savings from working at Finney's and Unnerstall's Drug Stores when he was in Central High School, to help pay for the education at St. Louis. The car he bought, after completion of the course of study, was a rather mundane

Chevy with a dark green body and a light green top. John kept this car immaculately clean but it had some flaws: the door on the passenger side would fling open when making a corner and I learned it was necessary to grasp the door handle in order to not fall out; also, after a few months of married life, we traveled to St. Louis to attend a pro basketball game returning in a down pouring rainstorm with water saturating my feet due to a leak at the seam of the windshield and dashboard. We traded the Chevy for a different and better vehicle within the first two years after we married.

- I did not know how to cook when we married. I assumed cooking would be easy for me since my Mother was an excellent cook. I had baked many cookies while at home but preparing full-fledged meals was something else. Fortunately John was not a picky eater and we subsisted on tuna casseroles and hamburgers, which resembled two-inch meatballs tucked between buns, for quite a while and were appreciative of eating with my folks as often as possible. (Actually my making a good meatloaf did not happen until around ten years into our marriage – I tried, and finally I found just the right ingredients for delicious results; my culinary skills became quite good).

- After we moved to Herrin, Illinois I learned from experience what clinkers were because the apartment, where we lived, was heated by coal

(coal was the main source for heating homes in the area). Periodically the furnace had to be replenished with fresh coal but first the residue, clinkers, had to be removed. For the most part we were comfortable and warm, if we followed through with the procedures. There was one exception: the laundry room was adjacent to the garage and was unheated. Southern Illinois winters can be frigid and once I was washing my usual dozens of diapers (before disposables) when the water pipes froze that were connected to the washer. The water from the pipes froze as soon as it hit the back wall and I remember wondering, as I was immersed dripping wet and freezing, what to do – nevertheless we lived through it all.

- I learned early to appreciate John's sense of humor, a trait that continued throughout our marriage. As illustration, one morning he telephoned me from the hospital lab (in Farmington} and asked me to bring an item for him. I complied but I needed to mail a letter before seeing him and proceeded with our two toddler little girls who were still wearing pajamas and bath robes. I knew about a drive-up mailbox, in front of a bank, and chose to drop the letter there. Unfortunately I misjudged and rammed the car into the mailbox relocating it about two feet. The incident created quite a commotion for the workers at the bank because the mailbox was close to the bank's entrance. No major damage was done to the car, the mailbox or anything else with the exception of my pride. John took great delight in telling me, "I heard someone needed to have a mailbox moved and I told them you could help." I seethed when he reminded me and, not until later, did I think there was any mirth to the incident.

- Out of necessity, sewing was a constant undertaking. The sewing machine helped create everything from children's clothing, clothing for me, curtains and various things. One late afternoon, when our daughters were probably around two and three years old, I decided to continue working on a slipcover for one of our chairs, while John was away playing softball. The process was going well until I started pushing material and piping under the sewing machine needle. Inadvertently, much to my dismay, I sewed my forefinger! In a split second I knew I had a predicament. The little girls could not help and no one else was with us. I impulsively turned the wheel which controlled the needle and my finger was released with half a sewing machine needle dangling from the finger nail – little blood was lost and all was well.

- John and I returned to academia by taking some night classes together. To say we had different notetaking styles is to put it mildly. I accumulated multiple note books from class lectures as opposed his using only one. The difference was simple: John had developed his own shorthand method which also meant I could not read his notes. However, I was pretty good at public speaking (I had made As in high school and college classes), at the time, and I critiqued his delivery of a presentation John did for U.S. History. The content, on early U.S. medical procedures, was very good but his eye contact during the speech was anything to be desired. Nonetheless, the outcome was an A for him and I ate "humble pie" afterwards.

- John admittedly could not sing well. This fact precipitated a joke about his singing the U.S. national anthem: his singing the anthem was not patriotic. John seized the opportunity to get back at his daughters after they and I had laughingly commented about a performance when he gave us his best vocal rendition. He took a tape recorder and allowed several minutes to pass before he bellowed, with much gusto, the anthem. That night he waited until his daughters were settled in their beds getting ready to sleep. At just an opportune time the quietness was permeated with a loud, "Oh, say can you see…." John was ecstatic when "Oh, Dad…" came from two sleepy girls. He had the last laugh and the response was worth it all for him.

- John was not a "Mr. Fixit" even though he often tried to be helpful; he excelled at sports and many other pursuits but I learned to do most things myself or hire someone else for the jobs. Over the years his attempts included: helping me wallpaper the kitchen and breakfast areas (I said the episode was a test of a good marriage because of the discord which developed); embarking on repairing a toilet, at midnight, and ultimately calling a plumber the next day; going to the dry cleaners on the same day he took the trash out to be collected and putting both bags of trash and items to be cleaned on the curb for pickup (later at the drycleaners he realized his mistake and frantically followed the garbage truck to the dump where the trash men graciously helped him find the bag with my favorite coat); once I visited Dawn and family in Virginia and I forgot to tell John about the refrigerator icemaker secret but he learned because of the overflowing ice cubes which he kept filling in buckets to be transported to our home's backyard (I can't imagine what the neighbors thought when they saw him with all that ice).

- I did not care for the "pomp and circumstance" which was required of me as faculty/staff for graduations at the community college where I was employed. Rain was a problem at one particular occasion. Everyone was seated at the out-of-doors event when unexpectedly a cloud burst resulted in a heavy deluge. Mortar boards were rendered into v-shaped umbrellas with water pouring on the participants. I was sitting with my soaked regalia, along with other staff and faculty, when I felt a tap on my shoulder – there stood John among all the people with an umbrella trying to protect me! He just wanted to be there for me in all kinds of weather no matter what.

- John always took advantage of occasions to show his caring for his family. Roses, boxes of Valentine hearts with chocolates, telephone calls when he was away, his infamous "bear hugs" along with the "surprise I love you notes" and so much more showed the value he placed on those he loved.

- One Christmas I took money I had earned from substitute teaching to buy John a really nice heavy and warm coat. At that time, we were living in St. Louis and John had to travel to Minnesota as well as other very cold destinations. I was concerned about his well-being. For many winters he carried the coat with him on trips. Later, after we moved to Arkansas, the coat remained a part of him even though it started to look weather worn – it took on more meaning than just to brace himself against the cold; he had become attached to the coat.

- John was competitive. He liked to win at whatever he did but, as he told me, he had no problem with a person who played a better game than he did (his desire for achievement probably stemmed from the American Legion award when he was in eighth grade – a source of pride for him). Along with other competitions, John loved chess.

One of the young men on the tennis team John coached at the college said he was the Arkansas state champion when was he was in high school and offered to play chess with John. The young man came to our house for snacks and eagerly sat down for an easy win. John, in a calm manner, proceeded to overcome his surprised opponent at each game. I really think John took some satisfaction from winning, from this recognized champion, but he showed no comeuppance to the student. John thought a competitor should be a good sport no matter what he played.

- Graduate school challenged both of us. The first summer, flooding of Missouri and Mississippi Rivers almost shut down the University of Missouri campus before the session was over and eventually made an ordinary six hour trip home into ten hours, incurring many extra miles to avoid flooded highways. Finally, after the long drive, John greeted me at our home with a big "welcome home" sign which reached across the driveway between two lawn chairs – he was glad I was home. But John never complained about having to take care of himself while I was gone; caked laundry detergent, when I found shirts in the hamper to be washed, told me how he struggled with his time on his on (I never mentioned to him what I saw on the shirts). However, the car incident was the topper. The last semester comps had to be taken in November at the main university campus. The day before the exams, I left Arkansas during mild temperatures but as I drove north the weather turned stormy as the colder temperatures plummeted. The next morning, after staying at a motel, I awakened to an ice-covered parking lot but I went on to the task awaiting at the university. The grueling six- hour comps passed and I started to go home. About an hour into the journey, while I was driving, a patch of ice on the road caused the car to spin out of control. Fortunately, no traffic was coming either direction on the two-lane highway. The car careened down a ditch, landing on an outer road. I breathed a sigh of relief as I prayed a prayer of gratitude. I continued on the last four hours of the trip. The car seemed fine and I decided to not worry John about what had happened. However the following Thursday, after John and I had gone to St. Louis and back, I came in from work when John said, "You want to tell what happened with the car." Reluctantly I recounted my little "mishap" which had unknowingly resulted in extensive damage to the underside of the car; John had learned about the damage later when an attendant at a service station looked at the car.

- Christmases always create memories. There was one Christmas that had an additional meaning apart from the usual joy and activities we celebrated with family. That year John and I found we were between visits from everyone;

one group came before Christmas and the other late on Christmas night. We took the chance to have brunch with a couple who attended church with us. We were involved in conversation, after enjoying a typical meal with quiche, muffins/ breads/ fruits etc., when someone rapped on our front door. I opened the door finding a woman with a tote bag brimming full of items, wrapped in Christmas paper, in each of her hands. Without hesitation she declared, "I need to go to Little Rock." I was stunned but immediately I went to the table where we had been eating. I told John about her. Both of us went back and invited her into our home. She told us she did not have regular custody of her children but a judge said she could see her son and daughter on Christmas if she could come to Little Rock (she randomly selected our house because of cars parked in our driveway). A counselor could arrange everything for the visit at a motel. She gave John a telephone number to call for verification of the story. John called the number. She was telling the truth. John and I looked at each other knowing this was what we had to do. We informed our guests. The trip was proceeded with the stranger in the back seat of the car. The counselor was waiting for us at the appointed motel. The woman left our car and we never saw or heard about her again. We didn't remember her name but I kept thinking about those bags of Christmas gifts and the anticipation of seeing her children on Christmas Day. Scripture says in Hebrews "…many have entertained angels unawares." Was she one of those angels? Maybe someday when I see John in heaven I will know.

- Many years ago I had a dream. The dream was beautiful with the appearance of an exquisite, tremendously large city, gleaming in light. John and I were awed by all the beauty from a far distance but as we observed the magnitude of the scene, we realized that it was more than either of us could fully comprehend. Finally, in the dream, I proclaimed, "John, that's the New Jerusalem." To which he replied, "So it is, Linda. So it is." Maybe I was given a glimpse of the future. I don't know. I have not experienced such a special vision since that night. However, I am thankful for the memory of the dream and the promise of being in the New Jerusalem in all its magnificent splendor with John and all the many others who will be there. Truly someday we will all be more than amazed.